Richard Garnett, Elizabeth Shelley, Percy Bysshe Shelley

Original Poetry by Victor and Cazire

Richard Garnett, Elizabeth Shelley, Percy Bysshe Shelley

Original Poetry by Victor and Cazire

ISBN/EAN: 9783337778217

Printed in Europe, USA, Canada, Australia, Japan

Cover: Foto ©Thomas Meinert / pixelio.de

More available books at **www.hansebooks.com**

·ORIGINAL
POETRY

BY

VICTOR & CAZIRE

[PERCY BYSSHE SHELLEY & ELIZABETH SHELLEY]

Edited by

RICHARD GARNETT

C.B., LL.D.

Published by

JOHN LANE, *at the Sign of the Bodley Head in* LONDON *and* NEW YORK

MDCCCXCVIII

INTRODUCTION

BETWEEN the completion of "*Queen Mab*" in 1813, and the composition of "*Alastor*" in 1815, Shelley underwent a silent internal revolution which transformed a vigorous writer in verse into a great original poet. Much the same transformation had previously occurred to Coleridge, but with this difference, that in the elder poet's case the metamorphosis is manifestly due in great measure to the influence of Wordsworth, but in Shelley's the impulse is wholly from within. The two poets, however, have this in common, that, unlike Wordsworth, Byron, and others who cannot claim to be enumerated among "the twice-born," from the period of their regeneration onward, their works are almost free from admixture with a prosaic element. Alone among the illustrious poetical reputations of their age, their fame would decidedly not be promoted by the suppression of any considerable proportion of their compositions after this crisis in their intellectual history. The test is an especially severe one as regards Shelley, not only because the actual bulk of his poetical work is so much greater than Coleridge's, but because he has triumphantly borne such an ordeal from the publication of mere fragments of it as has perhaps fallen to the lot of no other poet. Few indeed are the morsels collected in "The Relics of Shelley," and subsequently incorporated in his works, which a votary of his genius would part with for any consideration. They are not chips, but diamond dust.

In proportion, however, to the habitual excellence of Shelley's and Coleridge's work after the full development of their powers, is its inferiority in " the ages of ignorance." Shelley's beginnings are far the more unpromising, and every admirer of his genius must have frequently wished that the whole of his poetical production prior to "Queen Mab" could be bestowed as "alms for oblivion." Seldom have the beginnings of a poet been so destitute of merit as his early lyrics. Why, then, it may be asked, retrieve any more of them from obscurity? The question appears pertinent, but only to the uninitiated. The bibliographer and the book-hunter, no less than the Shelleian student, know that the recovery of the little book now republished from an unique copy is the final chapter of a romance, and a bibliographical event as rare as, according to Petrarch, the appearance of a Laura in heaven :—

> " *Quod optanti divûm promittere nemo*
> *Auderet.*"

The existence of a previously, unheard-of volume of poems by Shelley and an unknown coadjutor, published in 1810 under the title of " Original Poetry, by Victor and Cazire," was first announced by the present writer in an article entitled " Shelley in Pall Mall," in Macmillan's Magazine for June, 1860. The fact had been ascertained by himself when, in August or September 1859, in the exercise of what was then his ordinary duty, he placed a *newly purchased periodical entitled* Stockdale's Budget, *and published in* 1826–7, *on the shelves of the Library of the British Museum.* This Budget *was a scandalous periodical, in which the publisher Stockdale, who had been ruined by his publication of the still more scandalous "Memoirs of Harriet Wilson," sought to avenge himself upon society by raking together all the misdemeanours of the upper classes he could collect from the newspapers. Shelley was then commonly regarded as a social pariah, and fair game for a professional lampooner of the grade to which the once respectable publisher had sunk. Stockdale, remembering that he had letters from Shelley in his possession, began in the very first number of his* Budget *to utilise them for "copy," and make them the basis of a history of the acquaintance which had existed between the ill-matched pair in* 1810, *without, it must be said, any trace of unkindness to the poet, whom he seems to have appreciated as fully as possible for one who, although accidentally an Ishmaelite, was congenitally a Philistine. Thus the story of "Victor and Cazire" came to light. It shall be related in Stockdale's own words, with the retrenchment of some im-- material particulars.*

" *The unfortunate subject of these very slight recollections intro- duced himself to me early in the autumn of* 1810. *With anxiety in his countenance, he requested me to extricate him from a pecuniary difficulty in which he was involved with a printer, whose name I cannot call to mind, but who resided at Horsham. [Stockdale should have said Worthing.] I am not quite certain how the difference between the poet and the printer was arranged; but, after I had looked over the account I know that it was paid, though whether I assisted in the payment, by money or acceptance, I cannot remember.* *

" *Be that as it may, on the* 17th *September,* 1810, *I received fourteen hundred and eighty copies of a thin royal octavo volume in sheets. It was entitled, ' Original Poetry,' by Alonzo and Cazire, or two names something like them. The author told me that these poems were the joint production of himself and a friend, whose name was forgotten by me as soon as I heard it. I advertised the*

---

* *It is remarkable that Stockdale speaks of himself as the sole agent in the negotiation with Shelley, and ignores the existence of a senior partner in his father, who lived until* 1814. *It appears, from the memoir of the elder Stockdale in the " Dictionary of National Biography," that his business consisted largely in the purchase of " remainders," which may have facilitated the arrangement with the Worthing printer.*

*work, which was to be retailed at 3s. 6d., in nearly all the London papers of the day.**

"*Some short time after the announcement of the poems I happened to be perusing them, with more leisure than I had till then had leisure to bestow upon them, when I recognised one which I knew to have been written by Mr. M. G. Lewis, the author of ' The Monk,' and I fully anticipated the probable vexation of the juvenile author when I communicated my discovery to Mr. P. B. Shelley.*

"*With all the ardour natural to his character he expressed the warmest resentment at the imposition practised upon him by his coadjutor, and entreated me to destroy all the copies, of which about one hundred had been put into circulation.*"

Such is the history of " Victor and Cazire " according to Stockdale.   It was merely the prelude to an acquaintance of some duration between author and publisher, productive of interesting correspondence published in the Budget, *in* Macmillan's Magazine, *and in more than one edition of Shelley's letters.*

---

* *An advertisement of " Original Poetry," by Victor and Cazire, did in fact appear in the* Morning Chronicle *of September* 18, 1810, *the very day after Stockdale had received the copies.   The book was briefly reviewed in the* Poetical Register, *and Professor Dowden has unearthed a more ample, but by no means complimentary, notice in the* British Critic, *so late as April* 1811.

*One letter alone, however, concerns us now as re-
lating to " Victor and Cazire."*

" Field Place, Sept. 6, 1810.

" *Sir,*

"*I have to return you my thankful acknowledgment for
the receipt of the books, which arrived as soon as I had any
reason to expect; the superfluity shall be balanced as soon as I pay
for some books which I shall trouble you to bind for me.*

"*I enclose you the title-page of the Poems, which, as you will
see, you have mistaken on account of the illegibility of my hand-
writing. I have had the last proof-impression from my printer
this morning, and I suppose the execution of the work will not be
long delayed. As soon as it possibly can, it shall reach you, and
believe me, Sir, grateful for the interest you take in it.*

" I am, Sir,

" Your obedient, humble servant,

"PERCY B. SHELLEY."

It only remains to be added as regards the Budget
*that it is itself a book of great rarity; that the
Museum copy had been bought in January,* 1859 ;
*and that nothing can more conclusively show the
wisdom of purchasing everything for the national
library, however apparently unpromising. Not only
do we owe our knowledge of the very existence of
Shelley's first published volume of verse to this*

unsavoury publication, but without it the book might have turned up and passed from hand to hand without any suspicion of Shelley's authorship of anything in it occurring to any one.

Alice remarked in Wonderland that she had often seen a cat without a grin, but rarely a grin without a cat. It is common enough to find a book without a title, not so common to find a title without a book. The situation thus created for Shelleian book-hunters was a trying one. They were delivered from the peril of ignorance ; they were in no danger of passing a " Victor and Cazire" unheeded, or of trading it away. But to what end this unprofitable knowledge ? " De non existentibus et de non apparentibus eadem est ratio." The ardour of chase among Shelleians and book-hunters may be guessed, but " never can be wholly known." Some may have gone as far as that singularly determined character who once upon a time turned out the whole of Lacy's theatrical stock in quest of "Swellfoot the Tyrant," and got it. If any one was now equally resolute, he was not equally successful. Thirty-eight years elapsed ere the

destined knight appeared in the person of Mr. John
Lane, to whom the evasive volume was brought by
Mr. V. E. G. Hussey, the son of Mrs. Hussey, of
Quatrebras, Dorchester, herself a daughter of the
Rev. Charles Henry Grove, brother of the Harriet
Grove to whom many of the poems are addressed, and
who had been frequently, though, as we shall see,
erroneously, identified with " Cazire." Bound up
with the Third Canto of " Childe Harold," Byron's
"Corsair" and "Lara," and his "Lament of Tasso,"
and adorned with Mr. Grove's bookplate, the volume
had remained peacefully on his shelves since, perhaps,
1824. An inserted leaf bearing that date as a water
mark shows that it was not bound before that year,
nor, in all probability, very long afterwards.

Although the present scrupulously faithful and all
but facsimile reprint accurately reproduces the con-
tents of the volume, it may be convenient to enumerate
the pieces here, with numbers for the sake of refer-
ence.

1. Letter [Cazire].
2. Letter [Cazire].

3. *Song* [*Victor*].

4. *Song* [*Victor*].

5. *Despair* [*Victor*].

6. *Sorrow* [*Victor*].

7. *Hope* [*Victor*].

8. *Song translated from the Italian* [*probably Cazire*].

9. *Song translated from the German* [*doubtful*].

10. *The Irishman's Song* [*Victor*].

11. *Song* [*perhaps the plagiarised poem; if not, by Victor*].

12. *Song* [*Victor*].

13. *Song* [*Victor*].

14. *St. Edmona's Eve* [*doubtful*].

15. *Revenge* [*Victor; if not, a plagiarism*].

16. *Ghasta; or, the avenging Demon* [*Victor*].

17. *Fragment* [*reprinted as* "*Victoria*" *in* "*St. Irvyne*," *Victor*].

These seventeen pieces occupy sixty pages, and four more are devoted to the title-page and table of contents. The impression probably consisted of fifteen hundred copies, twenty of which would be retained by the writers. The copies sent to the newspapers must have been merely stitched in wrappers, and the same was probably the case with the presentation copy now recovered, or it would hardly have been bound up with other pamphlets. It is unlikely that nearly so many copies as the number stated by Stockdale were put into circulation.

The crudity of Shelley's early verse is too well known to permit the expectation of any accession to his fame from the discovery of so juvenile a production. There are, nevertheless, more points of interest in connection with the little volume than might have been expected, and to have apprehended these is to have in some measure extended our knowledge of the youthful Shelley. Our first business is to determine the identity of his coadjutor, and the extent of their respective participation in the book. The former of these investigations presents no difficulty. It has always been supposed that Cazire, probably borrowed from some French conte or novelette, must be a female name, and must denote either Shelley's sister

Elizabeth or his cousin and betrothed, Harriet Grove. There can now be no doubt on the former of these points, the second poem (To Miss ———, from Miss ———) being assuredly the composition of a young lady. The authorship is hardly less apparent, the poem in question being an epistle from one of the two cousins to the other, and the identity of the writer with Elizabeth Shelley appearing from the unmellifluous couplet:

> *" For they're all alike, take them one with another,*
> *Begging pardon—with the exception of my brother."*

The exception to the general demerit of masculine youth must clearly be the swain to whom the writer's friend is engaged; and as Harriet Grove was betrothed to Elizabeth Shelley's brother, not Elizabeth to Harriet's, the identity of the writer is fully established.*

The two initial pieces are the only two which can be attributed to Elizabeth Shelley with absolute

---

* Elizabeth Shelley never married. She died in December 1831, aged 37.

certainty, though others in the volume may possibly belong to her. Its contents may be classified thus :

1. *Familiar poems in the style of Anstey's " Bath Guide," the first two in the volume, already mentioned as by Elizabeth Shelley.*

2. *A cycle of little poems evidently addressea by Shelley to Harriet Grove, in the summer of* 1810. (*Nos.* 2–7, 12, 13.)

3. *Tales of terror and wonder in the style of Monk Lewis.* (*Nos.* 14–17.)

4. *A few miscellaneous pieces.* (*Nos.* 8–11.)

Elizabeth Shelley's vers de société *need no special characterisation. They are lively enough, and their occasional offences against grammar and metre are evidently due to the inexperience of the writer, who is not unaware of the necessity of frequent reference to the grammar and dictionary, though this does not save her from mistaking* arraign *for* arrange. *Considering, indeed, that Elizabeth Shelley was only seventeen, having been born on May* 10, 1794, *they evince quite as much finish as could be reasonably expected. The*

really interesting points are the allusion to the engage-
ment of the writer's brother to her cousin and
correspondent, and the hint of some distrust of its
stability. We have seen that the metrical epistle
must have been addressed to *Harriet Grove*, and the
blank in the line

"*Now your parcel's arrived* ——*'s letter shall go,*"

may be confidently filled up with Percy's *or* Bysshe's.
The name immediately excites the inauspicious aspira-
tion :

" *I hope all your joy mayn't be turned into woe,*"

a vein of thought pursued in several sequent lines,
evidently sincerely felt and much the best in the
piece.

These verses are dated *April* 30, 1810. Earlier
in the month Shelley had been with his lady-love, and
on parting from her had addressed to her the " *Song* "
(*No.* 4), artless lines not devoid of a touch of real
poetical quality. The blanks must of course be filled
with " *Harriet*," a name conducive to dactylic or ana-
paestic measures. The three following pieces, dated

in June and August, seem to adumbrate a misunder-standing and a reconciliation, such fallings in and out of love as would be likely to characterise the attachment of two such young people. On the whole, we seem to gain the impression that Shelley's feelings were more deeply interested than some of his biographers have allowed. He may well have thought of Harriet Grove when he afterwards wrote of Cosimo and Fiordispina :

> " *They were two cousins, almost like to twins,*
> *Except that from the catalogue of sins*
> *Nature had razed their love, which could not be,*
> *But by dissevering their nativity.*

This little cycle of love-verses, although with all its amazing incorrectness poetically the best section of the volume, exhibits so little affinity to Shelley's maturer style that it might have been attributed to his sister but for the unequivocal reference to Harriet Grove in the first of them, which there is no sufficient reason to separate from the others. A stanza, more-over, in the song to Hope (No. 7) :

"*The vermeil-tinted flowers that blossom*
Are frozen but to bud anew.
Then, sweet deceiver, calm my bosom,
Although thy visions be not true,"

seems to have been dimly present to Shelley's mind when he wrote, about 1817 :

"*Such is my heart : roses are fair,*
And that at best a withered blossom ;
But thy false care did idly wear
Its withered leaves in a faithless bosom."

The symbol of the frozen rose is also repeated in the same poem:

For the planet of frost, so cold and bright,
Makes it wan with her borrowed light."

The blank in the eighth line of another poem of this cycle (No. 12) must undoubtedly be filled by " Percy " or " Shelley."

We pass to another division of the poems in this little volume more characteristic than love-verses of the youthful Shelley—the tales of terror and wonder in the manner of Monk Lewis. Compositions in this taste, the first crude fruit of the Romantic School, in

England as everywhere else, preceded and preluded its really great achievements. England, indeed, had shown other nations the way with Horace Walpole's "Castle of Otranto," and when "Victor and Cazire" were beginning to sing, Anne Radcliffe, a writer of true genius, was usually considered the first living novelist. The taste of the day is thus pleasantly satirised by Miss Austen, not an authority to be suspected of gross exaggeration :

"When you have finished 'Udolpho,' we will read 'The Italian' together; and I have made out a list of ten or twelve more of the same kind for you."

"Have you, indeed? How glad I am! What are they all?"

"I will read you their names directly; here they are in my pocket-book. 'Castle of Wolfenbach,' 'Clermont,' 'Mysterious Warnings,' 'Necromancer of the Black Forest,' 'Midnight Bell,' 'Orphan of the Rhine,' and 'Horrid Mysteries.' Those will last us some time."

"Yes, pretty well; but are they all horrid? Are you sure they are all horrid?"

"Yes, quite sure."

("Northanger Abbey," ch. vi.)

It would have been strange indeed if a youth

of Shelley's enthusiastic temperament, who tells us that

> " *While yet a boy I sought for ghosts, and sped*
>   *Through many a listening chamber, cave, and ruin,*
>   *And starlight wood, with fearful steps pursuing*
>   *Hopes of high talk with the departed dead,"*

had failed to imbibe this general malady of his time. " His mind," says Medwin, who knew him well at this early period, " ran on bandits, castles, ruined towers, wild mountains, storms, and apparitions—the Terrific, which, according to Burke, is the great machinery of the Sublime." This is sufficiently evinced by his youthful romances, " Zastrozzi" and " St. Irvyne," and it is curious to remark that while withdrawing the rest of the " Victor and Cazire" volume, he reprinted one poem of this class, " Victoria," in the latter romance. Other pieces in " St. Irvyne" are composed in the same style, and, though equal rubbish in other respects, attest, like " Victoria," a dawning faculty for metre, and an appreciation of one of the most vigorous forms of the lyrical narrative, the stanza of Scott's " Helvellyn."

Had "Zastrozzi" and "St. Irvyne" never appeared, the pieces now reprinted would have possessed considerable literary and psychological interest ; but Shelley's early peculiarities have long been well known, and the only point of much curiosity in this department of the book would be the identification of the piece cribbed, as alleged by Stockdale, by Shelley's coadjutor from Monk Lewis. This we have been unable to effect, and must confess to some doubt whether Stockdale's testimony is entirely reliable. No piece in the volume seems half good enough to have been written by Monk Lewis, who, if not a highly inspired, is always a satisfactory writer, impressive in his tales of terror, and gracefully fluent in his Anacreontic vein. The first stanza of "Ghasta" is indeed an audacious plagiarism from Chatterton ; but it has long been known from Medwin that Shelley had written a poem with this title, and the appropriation of the stanza is especially noticed by the biographer. The coadjutor's appropriation may have been "Revenge" (No. 15), but this is hardly likely, for the motif *is nearly the same as* that of " Zastrozzi " ; while, though " Saint Edmond's Eve " is quite bad enough for her to have written, it is too bad for her to have stolen. Perhaps, on the whole, the plagiarism may most probably be identified with the song on Laura (No. 11), better worth stealing than most, but which we have not been able to trace in the writings of Lewis or else-where.

This really pretty poem falls into the miscellaneous section, which comprises Nos. 8–13. Of these the song from the Italian, whether really a translation or not, probably belongs to Elizabeth Shelley; the others we should be disposed to attribute to her brother. The most remarkable is " The Irishman's Song," which shows that Shelley's Irish sympathies were of very early date. They were in all proba-bility derived from the conversations on Catholic Emancipation which he must have been accustomed to hear at his father's. Arbitrary as Sir Timothy Shelley may have been in his personal behaviour, he was in politics a Whig and an ally of the Roman Catholic Duke of Norfolk. The home influences which surrounded Shelley's youth were distinctly favourable to the formation of Liberal opinions.

If these views are just, not more than five pieces in the volume, including the plagiarised poem, can be attributed to Elizabeth Shelley. The book is consequently a more important document for the mental history of Shelley than might have been expected, and enlarges our conception of Shelley's range at this early period, both of thought and of metrical practice. Childishly immature as it is, it offers nothing to forbid the anticipation of eventual excellence, and something to encourage it. It shows, at all events, that the youthful Shelley could write better verse than can be found in his novels, and that he even then possessed the feeling for melody which is rarely dissociated from more or less of endowment with the poetical faculty. Biographically, it contributes something to illustrate an obscure period of his life, and strengthens the belief that his attachment for his fair cousin was more than a passing fancy. It is, therefore, of considerable interest, apart from the romantic history which constitutes its chief claim to celebrity, and the *rarity which gives it a unique place among Shelley's extant writings. Fervently as we hoped that a copy might one day be found, we must now hope with equal fervour that no one may ever find another.*

It is incumbent upon the Editor to state that he assumes this function reluctantly, and only under compulsion from the gentleman by whom it ought to have been discharged. Mr. Money-Coutts, whose grandfather, Sir Francis Burdett, is mentioned in the second poem, had undertaken it at the instance of the publisher, and was proceeding with it most satisfactorily, when, learning that Mr. Garnett had been the means of making the existence of the poems known, he insisted that he should complete what he had begun by giving them to the world. The earnest remonstrances of Mr. Lane and Mr. Garnett failed to change the determination of Mr. Coutts, who persisted in an abnegation of the kind which Martial thought was only to be paralleled by the example of Virgil :

"*Would'st thou, my friend, essay the Muse, thou well*
Thy Martial's strain might'st equal or excel;
But, tender to a fault of my renown,

Thou art, Cyrenius, cruel to thine own.
Thus Maro, conscious of his might, forbore
Flaccus on lyric pinions to outsoar,
And, for the sake of Varius, seemed to scorn
The buskin he more worthily had worn.
Gifts, honour, service, friend from friend may claim;
But rare his friendship who resigns his fame.

There are Cyreniuses among us yet, and thus it comes to pass that the beginning of a third Metonic cycle finds the discoverer of Victor and Cazire's existence under these appellations in 1859 introducing their effusions to the British public in 1898.

R. GARNETT.

ORIGINAL POETRY;

BY

VICTOR AND CAZIRE.

CALL IT NOT VAIN :—THEY DO NOT ERR,

WHO SAY, THAT, WHEN THE POET DIES,

MUTE NATURE MOURNS HER WORSHIPPER.

Lay of the Last Minstrel.

WORTHING

PRINTED BY C. AND W. PHILLIPS,
FOR THE AUTHORS ;
AND SOLD BY J. J. STOCKDALE, 41, PALL-MALL,
AND ALL OTHER BOOKSELLERS.

1810.

CONTENTS.

ORIGINAL POETRY.

A Person complained that whenever he began to write, he never could arrange his ideas in grammatical order. Which occasion suggested the idea of the following lines :

HERE I sit with my paper, my pen and my ink,

First of this thing, and that thing, and t'other thing think ;

Then my thoughts come so pell-mell all into my mind,

That the sense or the subject I never can find :

This word is wrong placed,—no regard to the sense,

The present and future, instead of past tense,

Then my grammar I want ; O dear ! what a bore,

I think I shall never attempt to write more,

With patience I then my thoughts must arraign,

Have them all in due order like mutes in a train,

Like them too must wait in due patience and thought,

Or else my fine works will all come to nought.

My wit too's so copious, it flows like a river,

But disperses its waters on black and white never;

Like smoke it appears independent and free,

But ah luckless smoke! it all passes like thee—

Then at length all my patience entirely lost,

My paper and pens in the fire are tost;

But come, try again—you must never despair,

Our Murray's or Entick's are not all so rare,

Implore their assistance—they'll come to your aid,

Perform all your business without being paid,

They'll tell you the present tense, future and past,

Which should come first, and which should come last,

This Murray will do—then to Entick repair,

To find out the meaning of any word rare.

This they friendly will tell, and ne'er make you blush,

With a jeering look, taunt, or an O fie! tush!

Then straight all your thoughts in black and white put,

Not minding the if's, the be's, and the but,

Then read it all over, see how it will run,

How answers the wit, the retort, and the pun,

Your writings may then with old Socrates vie,

May on the same shelf with Demosthenes lie,

May as Junius be sharp, or as Plato be sage,

The pattern or satire to all of the age ;

But stop—a mad author I mean not to turn,

Nor with thirst of applause does my heated brain burn,

Sufficient that sense, wit, and grammar combined,

My letters may make some slight food for the mind ;

That my thoughts to my friends I may freely impart,

In all the warm language that flows from the heart,

Hark ! futurity calls ! it loudly complains,

It bids me step forward and just hold the reins,

My excuse shall be humble, and faithful, and true,

Such as I fear can be made but by few—

Of writers this age has abundance and plenty,

Three score and a thousand, two millions and twenty,

Three score of them wits who all sharply vie,

To try what odd creature they best can belie,

A thousand are prudes who for *Charity* write,

And fill up their sheets with spleen, envy, and spite

One million are bards, who to heaven aspire,

And stuff their works full of bombast, rant, and fire,

T'other million are wags who in Grub-street attend,

And just like a cobler the old writings mend,

The twenty are those who for pulpits indite,

And pore over sermons all Saturday night.

And now my good friends—who come after I mean,

As I ne'er wore a cassoc, or dined with a dean,

Or like coblers at mending I never did try,

Nor with poets in lyrics attempted to vie ;

As for prudes these good souls I both hate and detest,

So here I believe the matter must rest.—

I've heard your complaint—my answer I've made,

And since to your calls all the tribute I've paid,

Adieu my good friend ; pray never despair,

But grammar and sense and every thing dare,

Attempt but to write dashing, easy, and free,

Then take out your grammar and pay him his fee,

Be not a coward, shrink not to a tense,

But read it all over and make it out sense.

What a tiresome girl!—pray soon make an end,

Else my limited patience you'll quickly expend.

Well adieu, I no longer your patience will try—

So swift to the post now the letter shall fly.

JANUARY, 1810

To Miss ——— ———

From Miss ——— ———

———

For your letter, dear ———, accept my best thanks,

Rendered long and amusing by virtue of franks,

Tho' concise they would please, yet the longer the better,

The more news that's crammed in, more amusing the
    letter,

All excuses of etiquette nonsense I hate,

Which only are fit for the tardy and late,

As when converse grows flat, of the weather they talk,

How fair the sun shines—a fine day for a walk,

Then to politics turn, of Burdett's reformation,

One declares it would hurt, t'other better the nation,

Will ministers keep? sure they've acted quite wrong,

The burden this is of each morning—call song.

So —— is going to —— you say,

I hope that success her great efforts will pay

That —— will see her, be dazzled outright,

And declare he can't bear to be out of her sight.

Write flaming epistles with love's pointed dart,

Whose sharp little arrow struck right on his heart,

Scold poor innocent Cupid for mischevious ways,

He knows not how much to laud forth her praise,

That he neither eats, drinks or sleeps for her sake,

And hopes her hard heart some compassion will take,

A refusal would kill him, so desperate his flame,

But he fears, for he knows she is not common game,

Then praises her sense, wit, discernment and grace,

He's not one that's caught by a sly looking face,

Yet that's *too* divine—such a black sparkling eye,

At the bare glance of which near a thousand will die ;

Thus runs he on meaning but one word in ten,

More than is meant by most such kind of men,

For they're all alike, take them one with another,

Begging pardon—with the exception of my brother.

Of the drawings you mention much praise I have heard,

Most opinion's the same, with the difference of word,

Some get a good name by the voice of the crowd,

Whilst to poor humble merit small praise is allowed,

As in parliament votes, so in pictures a name,

Oft determines a fate at the altar of fame.—

So on Friday this City's gay vortex you quit,

And no longer with Doctors and Johnny cats sit—

Now your parcels arrived ———'s letter shall go,

I hope all your joy mayn't be turned into woe,

Experience will tell you that pleasure is vain,

When it promises sun shine how often comes rain.

So when to fond hope every blessing is nigh,

How oft when we smile it is checked with a sigh,

When Hope, gay deceiver, in pleasure is drest,

How oft comes a stroke that may rob us of rest.

When we think ourselves safe, and the gaol near at hand,

Like a vessel just landing, we're wrecked near the strand,

And tho' memory forever the sharp pang must feel,

'Tis our duty to bear, and our hardship to steel—

May misfortunes dear Girl, ne'er thy happiness cloy,

May thy days glide in peace, love, comfort and joy,

May thy tears with soft pity for other woes flow,

Woes, which thy tender heart never may know,

For hardships our own, God has taught us to bear,

Tho' sympathy's soul to a friend drops a tear.

Oh dear ! what sentimental stuff have I written,

Only fit to tear up and play with a kitten.

What sober reflections in the midst of this letter !

Jocularity sure would have suited much better ;

But there are exceptions to all common rules,

For this is a truth by all boys learnt at schools.

Now adieu my dear ———— I'm sure I must tire,

For if I do, you may throw it into the fire,

So accept the best love of your cousin and friend,

Which brings this nonsensical rhyme to an end

APRIL 30, 1810.

S O N G.

—————

Cold, cold is the blast when December is howling,

    Cold are the damps on a dying Man's brow,—

Stern are the seas when the wild waves are rolling,

    And sad is the grave where a loved one lies low ;

But colder is scorn from the being who loved thee,

More stern is the sneer from the friend who has proved

    thee,

More sad are the tears when their sorrows have moved thee,

    Which mixed with groans anguish and wild madness

    flow —

And ah ! poor ——— has felt all this horror,

    Full long the fallen victim contended with fate :

'Till a destitute outcast abandoned to sorrow,

    She sought her babe's food at her ruiners gate—

Another had charmed the remorseless betrayer,

He turned laughing aside from her moans and her prayer,

She said nothing, but wringing the wet from her hair,

　　Crossed the dark mountain side, tho' the hour it was

　　late.

'Twas on the wild height of the dark Penmanmawr,

　　That the form of the wasted ———— reclined ;

She shrieked to the ravens that croaked from afar,

　　And she sighed to the gusts of the wild sweeping wind.—

" I call not yon rocks where the thunder peals rattle,

" I call not yon clouds where the elements battle,

　　But thee, cruel ———— I call thee unkind !—

Then she wreathed in her hair the wild flowers of the

　　mountain,

　　And deliriously laughing, a garland entwined,

She bedewed it with tears, then she hung o'er the fountain,

　　And leaving it, cast it a prey to the wind.

" Ah ! go," she exclaimed, " when the tempest is yelling,

" 'Tis unkind to be cast on the sea that is swelling,

" But I left, a pityless outcast, my dwelling,

  " My garments are torn, so they say is my mind—"

Not long lived ———, but over her grave

  Waved the desolate form of a storm-blasted yew,

Around it no demons or ghosts dare to rave,

  But spirits of peace steep her slumbers in dew.

Then stay thy swift steps mid the dark mountain
    heather,

Tho' chill blow the wind and severe is the weather,

For perfidy, traveller ! cannot bereave her,

  Of the tears, to the tombs of the innocent due.—

                        JULY, 1810.

S O N G.

Come ——— ! sweet is the hour,
  Soft Zephyrs breathe gently around,
The anemone's night-boding flower,
  Has sunk its pale head on the ground.

'Tis thus the world's keenness hath torn,
  Some mild heart that expands to its blast,
'Tis thus that the wretched forlorn,
  Sinks poor and neglected at last.—

The world with its keenness and woe,
  Has no charms or attraction for me,
Its unkindness with grief has laid low,
  The heart which is faithful to thee.

The high trees that wave past the moon,

    As I walk in their umbrage with you,

All declare I must part with you soon,

    All bid you a tender adieu !—

Then ——— ! dearest farewell,

    You and I love, may ne'er meet again ;

These woods and these meadows can tell

    How soft and how sweet was the strain.—

APRIL, 1810.

S O N G.

D E S P A I R.

Ask not the pallid stranger's woe,

 With beating heart and throbbing breast,

Whose step is faultering, weak, and slow,

 As tho' the body needed rest.—

Whose wildered eye no object meets,

 Nor cares to ken a friendly glance,

With silent grief his bosom beats,—

 Now fixed, as in a deathlike trance.

Who looks around with fearful eye,

 And shuns all converse with mankind,

As tho' some one his griefs might spy,

 And soothe them with a kindred mind.

A friend or foe to him the same,

    He looks on each with equal eye;

The difference lies but in the name,

    To none for comfort can he fly.—

'Twas deep despair, and sorrow's trace,

    To him too keenly given,

Whose memory, time could not efface—

    His peace was lodged in Heaven.—

He looks on all this world bestows,

    The pride and pomp of power,

As trifles best for pageant shows

    Which vanish in an hour.

When torn is dear affections tie,

    Sinks the soft heart full low;

It leaves without a parting sigh,

    All that these realms bestow.

JUNE 1810.

SONG.

SORROW.

To me this world's a dreary blank,
    All hopes in life are gone and fled,
My high strung energies are sank,
    And all my blissfull hopes lie dead.—

The world once smiling to my view,
    Shewed scenes of endless bliss and joy ;
The world I then but little knew,
    Ah ! little knew how pleasures cloy ;

All then was jocund, all was gay,
    No thought beyond the present hour,
I danced in pleasures fading ray,
    Fading alas ! as drooping flower.

Nor do the heedless in the throng,

  One thought beyond the morrow give

They court the feast, the dance, the song,

  Nor think how short their time to live.

The heart that bears deep sorrows trace,

  What earthly comfort can console,

It drags a dull and lengthened pace,

  'Till friendly death its woes enroll.—

The sunken cheek, the humid eyes,

  E'en better than the tongue can tell;

In whose sad breast deep sorrow lies,

  Where memory's rankling traces dwell.—

The rising tear, the stifled sigh,

  A mind but ill at ease display,

Like blackening clouds in stormy sky,

  Where fiercely vivid lightening's play.

Thus when souls' energy is dead,

 When sorrow dims each earthly view,

When every fairy hope is fled,

 We bid ungrateful world adieu.

AUGUST 1810.

S O N G.

H O P E.

AND said I that all hope was fled,

    That sorrow and despair were mine,

That each enthusiast wish was dead,

    Had sank beneath pale Misery's shrine.—

Seest thou the sunbeam's yellow glow,

    That robes with liquid streams of light ;

You distant Mountain's craggy brow.

    And shews the rocks so fair,—so bright——

'Tis thus sweet expectations ray,

    In softer view shews distant hours,

And portrays each succeeding day,

    As dressed in fairer, brighter flowers,—

The vermiel tinted flowers that blossom ;

    Are frozen but to bud anew,

Then sweet deceivers calm my bosom,

    Although thy visions be not true,—

Yet true they are,—and I'll believe,

    Thy whisperings soft of love and peace,

God never made thee to deceive,

    'Tis sin that bade thy empire cease.

Yet tho' despair my life should gloom,

    Tho' horror should around me close,

With those I love, beyond the tomb,

    Hope shews a balm for all my woes.

AUGUST 1810.

SONG.

TRANSLATED FROM THE ITALIAN.

Oh! what is the gain of restless care,

    And what is ambitious treasure?

And what are the joys that the modish share,

    In their sickly haunts of pleasure?

My husbands repast with delight I spread,

    What tho' 'tis but rustic fare,

May each guardian angel protect his shed,

    May contentment and quiet be there.

And may I support my husbands years,

    May I soothe his dying pain,

And then may I dry my fast falling tears,

    And meet him in Heaven again.

JULY, 1810.

SONG.

TRANSLATED FROM THE GERMAN.

Ah! grasp the dire dagger and couch the fell spear,
If vengeance and death to thy bosom be dear,
The dastard shall perish, deaths torment shall prove,
For fate and revenge are decreed from above.

Ah! where is the hero, whose nerves strung by youth,
Will defend the firm cause of justice and truth;
With insatiate desire whose bosom shall swell,
To give up the oppressor to judgment and Hell—

For him shall the fair one twine chaplets of bays,
To him shall each warrior give merited praise,
And triumphant returned from the clangor of arms,
He shall find his reward in his loved maidens charms.

In extatic confusion the warrior shall sip,

The kisses that glow on his love's dewy lip,

And mutual, eternal, embraces shall prove,

The rewards of the brave are the transports of love.

OCTOBER, 1809.

THE IRISHMAN'S SONG.

THE stars may dissolve, and the fountain of light

May sink into ne'er ending chaos and night,

Our mansions must fall, and earth vanish away,

But thy courage O Erin! may never decay.

See! the wide wasting ruin extends all around,

Our ancestors dwellings lie sunk on the ground,

Our foes ride in triumph throughout our domains,

And our mightiest heroes lie stretched on the plains.

Ah! dead is the harp which was wont to give pleasure,

Ah! sunk is our sweet country's rapturous measure,

But the war note is waked, and the clangor of spears,

The dread yell of Sloghan yet sounds in our ears.

Ah! where are the heroes! triumphant in death,

Convulsed they recline on the blood sprinkled heath,

Or the yelling ghosts ride on the blast that sweeps by,

And "my countrymen! vengeance!" incessantly cry.

OCTOBER, 1809.

SONG.

Fierce roars the midnight storm
  O'er the wild mountain,
Dark clouds the night deform,
  Swift rolls the fountain—

See ! o'er yon rocky height,
  Dim mists are flying—
See by the moon's pale light,
  Poor Laura's dying !

Shame and remorse shall howl,
  By her false pillow—
Fiercer than storms that roll,
  O'er the white billow ;

No hand her eyes to close,

    When life is flying,

But she will find repose,

    For Laura's dying!

Then will I seek my love,

    Then will I cheer her,

Then my esteem will prove,

    When no friend is near her.

On her grave I will lie,

    When life is parted,

On her grave I will die,

    For the false hearted.

DECEMBER, 1809.

S O N G.

To —————————

Ah! sweet is the moonbeam that sleeps on yon fountain,
  And sweet the mild rush of the soft-sighing breeze,
And sweet is the glimpse of yon dimly-seen mountain,
  'Neath the verdant arcades of yon shadowy trees.

But sweeter than all was thy tone of affection,
  Which scarce seemed to break on the stillness of eve,
Though the time it is past!—yet the dear recollection,
  For aye in the heart of thy ——— must live.

Yet he hears thy dear voice in the summer winds sighing,
  Mild accents of happiness lisp in his ear,
When the hoped-winged moments athwart him are flying,
  And he thinks of the friend to his bosom so dear.—

And thou dearest friend in his bosom for ever

    Must reign unalloyed by the fast rolling year,

He loves thee, and dearest one never, Oh ! never

    Canst thou cease to be loved by a heart so sincere.

                              AUGUST, 1810.

SONG.

To ———————

Stern, stern is the voice of fates fearfull command,

    When accents of horror it breathes in our ear,

Or compels us for aye bid adieu to the land,

    Where exists that loved friend to our bosom so dear,

'Tis sterner than death o'er the shuddering wretch bending,

And in skeleton grasp his fell sceptre extending,

Like the heart-stricken deer to that loved covert wending,

    Which never again to his eyes may appear—

And ah ! he may envy the heart-stricken quarry,

    Who bids to the friend of affection farewell,

He may envy the bosom so bleeding and gory,

    He may envy the sound of the drear passing knell,

Not so deep is his grief on his death couch reposing,

When on the last vision his dim eyes are closing!

As the outcast whose love-raptured senses are losing,

The last tones of thy voice on the wild breeze that

swell!

Those tones were so soft, and so sad, that ah! never,

Can the sound cease to vibrate on Memory's ear,

In the stern wreck of Nature for ever and ever,

The remembrance must live of a friend so sincere.

AUGUST, 1810.

SAINT EDMOND'S EVE.

———

Oh ! did you observe the black Canon pass,
   And did you observe his frown ?
He goeth to say the midnight mass,
   In holy St. Edmond's town.

He goeth to sing the burial chaunt,
   And to lay the wandering sprite,
Whose shadowy, restless form doth haunt,
   The Abbey's drear aisle this night.

It saith it will not its wailing cease,
   'Till that holy man come near,
'Till he pour o'er its grave the prayer of peace,
   And sprinkle the hallowed tear.

The Canon's horse is stout and strong
    The road is plain and fair,
But the Canon slowly wends along,
    And his brow is gloomed with care.

Who is it thus late at the Abbey-gate?
    Sullen echoes the portal bell,
It sounds like the whispering voice of fate,
    It sounds like a funeral knell.

The Canon his faultering knee thrice bowed,
    And his frame was convulsed with fear,
When a voice was heard distinct and loud,
    " Prepare! for thy hour is near."

He crosses his breast, he mutters a prayer,
    To Heaven he lifts his eye,
He heeds not the Abbot's gazing stare,
    Nor the dark Monks who murmured by.

Bare-headed he worships the sculptured saints
   That frown on the sacred walls,
His face it grows pale,—he trembles, he faints,
   At the Abbot's feet he falls.

And strait the father's robe he kissed,
   Who cried, " Grace dwells with thee,
" The spirit will fade like the morning mist,
    " At your benedicite.

" Now haste within ! the board is spread,
   "Keen blows the air, and cold,
" The spectre sleeps in its earthy bed,
    " 'Till St. Edmond's bell hath tolled,—

" Yet rest your wearied limbs to-night,
   " You've journeyed many a mile,
" To-morrow lay the wailing sprite,
    " That shrieks in the moonlight aisle.

"Oh ! faint are my limbs and my bosom is cold,

" Yet to-night must the sprite be laid,

" Yet to-night when the hour of horror's told,

" Must I meet the wandering shade.

" Nor food, nor rest may now delay,—

" For hark ! the echoing pile,

" A bell loud shakes!—Oh haste away,

" O lead to the haunted aisle."

The torches slowly move before,

The cross is raised on high,

A smile of peace the Canon wore,

But horror dimmed his eye—

And now they climb the footworn stair,

The chapel gates unclose,

Now each breathed low a fervent prayer,

And fear each bosom froze——

Now paused awhile the doubtful band
　　And viewed the solemn scene,—
Full dark the clustered columns stand,
　　The moon gleams pale between—

" Say father, say, what cloisters gloom
　　" Conceals the unquiet shade,
" Within what dark unhallowed tomb,
　　" The corse unblessed was laid."

" Through yonder drear aisle alone it walks,
　　And murmurs a mournful plaint,
Of thee ! Black Canon, it wildly talks,
　　And call on thy patron saint—

" The pilgrim this night with wondering eyes,
　　" As he prayed at St. Edmond's shrine,
" From a black marble tomb hath seen it rise,
　　" And under yon arch recline."—

" Oh ! say upon that black marble tomb,

   " What memorial sad appears."—

" Undistinguished it lies in the chancels gloom,

   " No memorial sad it bears "—

The Canon his paternoster reads,

   His rosary hung by his side,

Now swift to the chancel door he leads,

   And untouched they open wide,

Resistless, strange sounds his steps impel,

   To approach to the black marble tomb,

" Oh ! enter Black Canon " a whisper fell,

   "Oh ! enter, thy hour is come."

He paused, told his beads, and the threshold passed,

   Oh ! horror, the chancel doors close,

A loud yell was borne on the rising blast,

   And a deep, dying groan arose.

The Monks in amazement shuddering stand,

    They burst thro' the chancels gloom,

From St. Edmond's shrine, lo ! a skeletons hand,

    Points to the black marble tomb.

Lo ! deeply engraved, an inscription blood red,

    In characters fresh and clear—

" The guilty black Canon of Elmham's dead,

    " And his wife lies buried here !"

In Elmham's tower he wedded a Nun,

    To St. Edmond's his bride he bore,

On this eve her noviciate here was begun,

    And a monks grey weeds she wore ;—

O ! deep was her conscience dyed with guilt,

    Remorse she full oft revealed,

Her blood by the ruthless black Canon was spilt,

    And in death her lips he sealed ;

Her spirit to penance this night was doomed,

    'Till the Canon atoned the deed,

Here together they now shall rest entombed,

    'Till their bodies from dust are freed—

Hark ! a loud peal of thunder shakes the roof,

    Round the altar bright lightnings play,

Speechless with horror the monks stand aloof,

    And the storm dies sudden away—

The inscription was gone ! a cross on the ground,

    And a rosary shone thro' the gloom,

But never again was the Canon there found,

    Or the Ghost on the black marble tomb.

REVENGE.

———

" Ah ! quit me not yet, for the wind whitsles shrill,

" Its blast wanders mournfully over the hill,

" The thunders wild voice rattles madly above,

" You will not then, cannot then, leave me my love.—"

" I must dearest Agnes, the night is far gone—

" I must wander this evening to Strasburg alone,

" I must seek the drear tomb of my ancestors bones,

" And must dig their remains from beneath the cold stones.

" For the spirit of Conrad there meets me this night,

" And we quit not the tomb 'till dawn of the light,

" And Conrad's been dead just a month and a day !

" So farewell dearest Agnes for I must away,—

" He bid me bring with me what most I held dear,

" Or a month from that time should I lie on my bier,

" And I'd sooner resign this false fluttering breath,

" Than my Agnes should dread either danger or death,

" And I love you to madness my Agnes I love,

" My constant affection this night will I prove,

" This night will I go to the sepulchres jaw,

" Alone will I glut its all conquering maw "—

" No ! no loved Adolphus thy Agnes will share,

" In the tomb all the dangers that wait for you there,

" I fear not the spirit,—I fear not the grave,

" My dearest Alolphus I'd perish to save " —

" Nay seek not to say that thy love shall not go,

" But spare me those ages of horror and woe,

" For I swear to thee here that I'll perish ere day,

" If you go unattended by Agnes away "—

The night it was bleak the fierce storm raged around,

The lightnings blue fire-light flashed on the ground,

Strange forms seemed to flit,—and howl tidings of fate,

As Agnes advanced to the sepulchre gate.—

The youth struck the portal,—the echoing sound

Was fearfully rolled midst the tombstones around,

The blue lightning gleamed o'er the dark chapel spire,

And tinged were the storm clouds with sulphurous fire.

Still they gazed on the tombstone where Conrad reclined,

Yet they shrank at the cold chilling blast of the wind,

When a strange silver brilliance pervaded the scene,

And a figure advanced—tall in form—fierce in mien.

A mantle encircled his shadowy form,

As light as a gossamer borne on the storm,

Celestial terror sat throned in his gaze,

Like the midnight pestiferous meteors blaze.—

SPIRIT.

Thy father, Adolphus! was false, false as hell,

And Conrad has cause to remember it well,

He ruined my Mother, despised me his son,

I quitted the world ere my vengeance was done.

I was nearly expiring—'twas close of the day,—

A demon advanced to the bed where I lay,

He gave me the power from whence I was hurled,

To return to revenge, to return to the world,—

Now Adolphus I'll seize thy best loved in my arms,

I'll drag her to Hades all blooming in charms,

On the black whirlwinds thundering pinion I'll ride,

And fierce yelling fiends shall exult o'er thy bride—

He spoke, and extending his ghastly arms wide,

Majestic advanced with a swift noiseless stride,

He clasped the fair Agnes—he raised her on high,

And cleaving the roof sped his way to the sky—

All was now silent,—and over the tomb,

Thicker, deeper, was swiftly extended a gloom,

Adolphus in horror sank down on the stone,

And his fleeting soul fled with a harrowing groan.

DECEMBER 1809.

G H A S T A ;

OR, THE AVENGING DEMON ! ! !

---

*The idea of the following tale was taken from a few un-
connected German Stanzas.—The principal Character is
evidently the Wandering Jew, and although not mentioned
by name, the burning Cross on his forehead undoubtedly al-
ludes to that superstition, so prevalent in the part of Germany
called the Black Forest, where this scene is supposed to lie.*

Hark ! the owlet flaps her wing,

In the pathless dell beneath,

Hark ! night ravens loudly sing,

Tidings of despair and death.—

Horror covers all the sky,

Clouds of darkness blot the moon,

Prepare ! for mortal thou must die,

Prepare to yield thy soul up soon—

Fierce the tempest raves around,

    Fierce the volleyed lightnings fly,

Crashing thunder shakes the ground,

    Fire and tumult fill the sky.—

Hark ! the tolling village bell,

    Tells the hour of midnight come,

Now can blast the powers of Hell,

    Fiend-like goblins now can roam—

See ! his crest all stained with rain,

    A warrior hastening speeds his way,

He starts, looks round him, starts again,

    And sighs for the approach of day.

See ! his frantic steed he reigns,

    See ! he lifts his hands on high,

Implores a respite to his pains,

    From the powers of the sky.—

He seeks an Inn, for faint from toil,

    Fatigue had bent his lofty form,

To rest his wearied limbs awhile,

    Fatigued with wandering and the storm.

    ※   ※   ※   ※   ※   ※   ※

    ※   ※   ※   ※   ※   ※   ※

Slow the door is opened wide—

    With trackless tread a stranger came,

His form Majestic, slow his stride,

    He sate, nor spake,—nor told his name—

Terror blaunched the warrior's cheek,

    Cold sweat from his forehead ran,

In vain his tongue essayed to speak,——

    At last the stranger thus began :

" Mortal ! thou that saw'st the sprite,

    " Tell me what I wish to know,

" Or come with me before 'tis light,

    " Where cypress trees and mandrakes grow.

" Fierce the avenging Demon's ire,

 " Fiercer than the wintry blast,

" Fiercer than the lightnings fire,

 " When the hour of twilights past—

The warrior raised his sunken eye,

 It met the stranger's sullen scowl,

" Mortal! Mortal! thou must die,"

 In burning letters chilled his soul.

WARRIOR.

" Stranger! whoso'er you are,

 I feel impelled my tale to tell—

Horrors stranger shalt thou hear,

 Horrors drear as those of Hell.

O'er my Castle silence reigned,

 Late the night and drear the hour,

When on the terrace I observed,

 A fleeting shadowy mist to lower.—

Light the cloud as summer fog,

   Which transient shuns the morning beam ;

Fleeting as the cloud on bog,

   That hangs or on the mountain stream.—

Horror seized my shuddering brain,

   Horror dimmed my starting eye,

In vain I tried to speak,—In vain

   My limb's essayed the spot to fly—

At last the thin and shadowy form,

   With noiseless, trackless footsteps came,—

Its light robe floated on the storm,

   Its head was bound with lambent flame.

In chilling voice drear as the breeze

   Which sweeps along th' autumnal ground,

Which wanders thro' the leafless trees,

   Or the mandrakes groan which floats around.

"Thou art mine and I am thine,

 "'Till the sinking of the world,

"I am thine and thou art mine,

 "'Till in ruin death is hurled——

"Strong the power and dire the fate

 "Which drags me from the depths of Hell,

"Breaks the tombs eternal gate,

 "Where fiendish shapes and dead men yell.

"Haply I might ne'er have shrank

 "From flames that rack the guilty dead,

"Haply I might ne'er have sank

 "On pleasures flowry, thorny bed—

—"But stay ! no more I dare disclose,

 "Of the tale I wish to tell,

"On Earth relentless were my woes,

 "But fiercer are my pangs in Hell--

" Now I claim thee as my love,

    " Lay aside all chilling fear,

" My affection will I prove,

    " Where sheeted ghosts and spectres are !

" For thou art mine, and I am thine,

    " 'Till the dreaded judgment day,

" I am thine, and thou art mine—

    " Night is past—I must away."

Still I gazed, and still the form

    Pressed upon my aching sight,

Still I braved the howling storm,

    When the ghost dissolved in night.—

Restless, sleepless fled the night,

    Sleepless as a sick mans bed,

When he sighs for morning light,

    When he turns his aching head,—

Slow and painful passed the day,

 Melancholy seized my brain,

Lingering fled the hours away,

 Lingering to a wretch in pain.—

At last came night, ah ! horrid hour,

 Ah ! chilling time that wakes the dead,

When demons ride the clouds that lower,

 —The phantom sat upon my bed.

In hollow voice, low as the sound

 Which in some charnel makes it moan,

What floats along the burying ground,

 The phantom claimed me as her own.

Her chilling finger on my head,

 With coldest touch congealed my soul—

Cold as the finger of the dead,

 Or damps which round a tombstone roll—

Months are passed in lingering round,

    Every night the spectre comes,

With thrilling step it shakes the ground,

    With thrilling step it round me roams—

Stranger! I have told to thee,

    All the tale I have to tell—

Stranger! canst thou tell to me,

    How to 'scape the powers of Hell"—

STRANGER.

Warrior! I can ease thy woes,

    Wilt thou, wilt thou, come with me—

Warrior! I can all disclose,

    Follow, follow, follow me.

Yet the tempests duskiest wing,

    Its mantle stretches o'er the sky,

Yet the midnight ravens sing,

    " Mortal! Mortal thou must die."

At last they saw a river clear,

  That crossed the heathy path they trode,

The Stranger's look was wild and drear,

  The firm Earth shook beneath his nod—

He raised a wand above his head,

  He traced a circle on the plain,

In a wild verse he called the dead,

  The dead with silent footsteps came.

A burning brilliance on his head,

  Flaming filled the stormy air,

In a wild verse he called the dead,

  The dead in motley crowd were there.—

" Ghasta ! Ghasta ! come along,

  " Bring thy fiendish crowd with thee,

" Quickly raise th' avenging Song,

  "Ghasta ! Ghasta ! come to me."

Horrid shapes in mantles grey,

   Flit athwart the stormy night,

" Ghasta ! Ghasta ! come away,

   " Come away before 'tis light."

See ! the sheeted Ghost they bring,

   Yelling dreadful o'er the heath,

Hark ! the deadly verse they sing,

   Tidings of despair and death !

The yelling Ghost before him stands,

   See ! she rolls her eyes around,

Now she lifts her bony hands,

   Now her footsteps shake the ground.

STRANGER.

Phantom of Theresa say,

   Why to earth again you came,

Quickly speak, I must away !

   Or you must bleach for aye in flame,—

PHANTOM.

" Mighty one I know thee now,

  " Mightiest power of the sky,

" Know thee by thy flaming brow,

  " Know thee by thy sparkling eye.

" That fire is scorching! Oh! I came,

  " From the caverned depth of Hell,

" My fleeting false Rodolph to claim,

  " Mighty one! I know thee well."—

STRANGER.

Ghasta! seize yon wandering sprite,

  Drag her to the depth beneath,

Take her swift, before 'tis light,

  Take her to the cells of death!

Thou that heardst the trackless dead,

  In the mouldering tomb must lie,

Mortal! look upon my head,

  Mortal! Mortal! thou must die.

Of glowing flame a cross was there,

　　Which threw a light around his form,

Whilst his lank and raven hair,

　　Floated wild upon the storm.—

The warrior upwards turned his eyes,

　　Gazed upon the cross of fire,

There sat horror and surprise,

　　There sat God's eternal ire.—

A shivering through the Warrior flew,

　　Colder than the nightly blast,

Colder than the evening dew,

　　When the hour of twilights past.—

Thunder shakes th' expansive sky,

　　Shakes the bosom of the heath,

" Mortal ! Mortal ! thou must die "—

　　The warrior sank convulsed in death.

JANUARY, 1810.

FRAGMENT,

OR THE TRIUMPH OF CONSCIENCE.

———•———

'Twas dead of the night when I sate in my dwelling,

  One glimmering lamp was expiring and low,—

Around the dark tide of the tempest was swelling,

Along the wild mountains night-ravens were yelling,

  They bodingly presaged destruction and woe !

'Twas then that I started, the wild storm was howling,

  Nought was seen, save the lightning that danced on

    the sky,

Above me the crash of the thunder was rolling,

  And low, chilling murmurs the blast wafted by.—

My heart sank within me, unheeded the jar

  Of the battling clouds on the mountain tops broke,

Unheeded the thunder-peal crashed in mine ear,

This heart hard as iron was stranger to fear,

But conscience in low noiseless whispering spoke.

'Twas then that her form on the whirlwind uprearing,

The dark ghost of the murdered Victoria strode,

Her right hand a blood reeking dagger was bearing,

She swiftly advanced to my lonesome abode.—

I wildly then called on the tempest to bear me !

     *   *   *   *   *   *   *   *

*   *   *   *   *   *   *   *

PHILLIPS, PRINTERS, WORTHING.

NOTES

Page 10—The blanks in the heading of this letter are no doubt to be filled up, "To Miss Harriet Grove from Miss Elizabeth Shelley." Those in the first line, and in the last but three, to be supplied with "Harrie," or "Hattie"; and that on *page* 12, *line* 9, with "Percy's," or "Bysshe's."

In *line* 9 of *page* 10 the name Burdett is so placed as to require the accentuation of the second syllable instead of the first, upon which the stress ought to fall.

Page 11, *line* 1.

So ——— is going to ——— you say.

The first blank is probably to be filled by the name of Harriet Grove's sister, for Harriet wrote in her diary on September 17, 1810, "Received the poetry by Victor and Cazire. C. offended, and with reason. I think they have done very wrong in publishing what they have of her."

E

Perhaps this displeasure on the young lady's part, and her sister's, may have been one reason for the suppression of the book.

Page 11, *line* 3—The word left blank was printed, but has been erased.

Page 12, *lines* 7, 8.

> *So on Friday this City's gay vortex you quit,*
> *And no longer with Doctors and Johnny cats sit.*

These lines are explained by a passage in Harriet Grove's diary :

"April 21, 1810.—Got to John's ; found him and his cat perfectly well, and happy to see us as we are to see him." John Grove followed the medical profession, and at that time lived in Lincoln's Inn.

There are no other passages in Miss Grove's diary referring to Victor and Cazire directly or indirectly.

Ibid, line 9—For *parcels* read *parcel's.*

Ibid—Four lines from bottom, for *gaol* read *goal.*

Page 19, *line* 5—The blank is to be filled with *Harriet.*

Page 22, *at bottom*—For *lightening's* read *lightnings.*

Page 25, *line* 3—For *deceivers* read *deceiver.*

Page 33, *line* 8—Blank to be filled by "Percy" or "Shelley."

" *Page* 45, *line* 1—For *whitsles* read *whistles.*

www.ingramcontent.com/pod-product-compliance
Lightning Source LLC
Chambersburg PA
CBHW020039030726

47499CB00007B/2495